little hands
SEEDS

RACHEL MATTHEWS

Chrysalis Children's Books

All kinds of plants grow from seeds.

Seeds grow into trees,
flowers, fruit and vegetables.

Seeds vary in size, shape, weight and colour.

orange

radish

apple

cherry

cress

grape

4

Collect some different seeds.
What do they look and feel like?

marigold

oak (acorn)

plum

horse chestnut (conker)

sycamore

5

Pour small seeds into a pot with a lid.

Put large seeds in another pot.

What colour and shape are the seeds?

Shake each pot.

What different sounds do the seeds inside make?

The outside of this seed is smooth and firm.

Inside this seed is a tiny plant waiting to grow.

What happens when you plant a seed?

Put a seed in a pot of damp soil. Gently cover the seed with soil.

Put the pot in a light place.
Make sure the soil stays damp.

A plant is beginning to grow from the seed!
Can you see the green shoot?

Roots grow down from the seed.

A growing plant
sucks up water
through its roots.

13

When a plant has flowered it leaves seeds behind.

Often the seeds are
protected inside a
fruit or pod.

This runner
bean holds the
seeds inside.

Collect some fruits and vegetables. Look inside them.

cucumber

kiwi fruit

pear

tomato

pomegranate

Some have many tiny seeds. Others have just one big seed.

avocado

cherry

papaya

pepper

squash

Plants scatter
their seeds in
different ways.

Light seeds
are blown by
the wind.

Seeds are food for many animals.
They spread seeds by storing and eating them.

People eat seeds, too.

We cook with them and eat them raw.

Which of these seeds have you tasted?

coffee

poppy

sunflower

orchid (vanilla)

rice

sesame

pumpkin

Make a seed-cake for birds to eat.

Stir some seeds
into melted
vegetable fat.
Ask an adult
to help you.

Notes for teachers and parents

Pages 2–3
Discussion: Encourage the children to discuss their experience of seeds. They may have noticed sesame seeds on top of hamburger buns or have a pet hamster that eats seeds. They may prefer seedless grapes to grapes with pips inside.
Activity: To introduce the connection between seeds and the germination and growth of flowering plants, you could invite a gardener to talk to the children about growing plants from seed. You could plant some seeds in the classroom. The children could make and illustrate their own seed packets.

Pages 4–5
Seeds can vary greatly in size, shape and appearance, eg. a conker in its spiky case is a seed, as is a pea in a pod, an avocado stone and an orange pip.
Activity: Collect examples of seeds and ask the children to describe each one and explain how it differs from another, eg. "This seed is round, smooth, shiny and brown and that seed is smaller and flatter and it's green."

Pages 6-7
Activity: If available, let the children experiment with musical instruments that use seeds to make sounds, eg. coconut shells, shakers and rainmakers (seed-filled tubes which replicate the sound of falling rain).

Pages 8–9
Explain that a seed's hard outer layer protects the plant inside it which will begin to grow when the conditions are right.
Experiment: Soak a bean seed overnight, remove its outer coating and cut it open to show children the embryonic plant inside.

Pages 10–13
Planting seeds allows children to explore the conditions necessary for germination.
Activity: Cress seeds germinate reliably and can be grown on damp blotting paper so the children can see what is happening. Each child could try planting some seeds in the shape of his or her name or initials.
Experiment: Investigate what happens when seeds are left unwatered. Encourage the children to deduce that water is needed for seeds to germinate. Put one set of germinated seeds on a window sill and another in a dark cupboard. Comparing the progress of the two sets, the children should notice that plants need light as well as water to grow and flourish.

Pages 14–17
Introduce the idea of a life cycle of a flowering plant, from seed to flower to seed-filled "fruit".
Activity: Show the children a flowering plant (removed from its pot), and point out the different parts: roots, stem, leaves and the flowers with their petals.
Activity: Show the children the "ripe" seed pod (the fruit) of a plant such as a petunia. The children could try shaking the pod over a paper bag to collect the seeds.

Pages 18–19
Link the need for a plant to spread its seeds to its life cycle.
Discussion: Study a range of seeds, eg. on a dandelion head, in a poppy seed-head, inside a melon or on the surface of a strawberry. Can the children suggest some ways in which the seeds might be dispersed?

Pages 20–22
Many seeds are good for us as they contain healthy food for a growing plant.
Activity: Make a list of seeds the children have come across at home and at school. Point out ones that the children may not have thought of as seeds, such as coffee and rice.
Discussion: Remind the children that not all seeds are safe to eat and tell them to check with an adult before touching or tasting any seeds that are new to them.

Index

First published in the UK in 2005 by
Chrysalis Children's Books
An imprint of Chrysalis Books Group Plc
The Chrysalis Building, Bramley Road
London W10 6SP

ISBN 1 84458 178 0

British Library Cataloguing in Publication Data for this book is available
from the British Library.

Associate publisher Joyce Bentley
Project manager and editor Penny Worm
Art director Sarah Goodwin
Designer Patricia Hopkins
Picture researchers Veneta Bullen, Miguel Lamas
Photographer Ray Moller

The author and publishers would like to thank the following people for their contributions
to this book: Ruth Thomson, Jack Bell, Mollie Worms and Mollie Parker.

Printed in China

10 9 8 7 6 5 4 3 2 1

Typography Natascha Frensch

Read Regular, READ SMALLCAPS and Read Space; European Community
Design Registration 2003 and Copyright © Natascha Frensch 2001-2004
Read Medium, **Read Black** and *Read Slanted* Copyright © Natascha Frensch
2003-2004

READ™ is a revolutionary new typeface that will enhance children's understanding
through clear, easily recognisable character shapes. With its evenly spaced and
carefully designed characters, READ™ will help children at all stages to improve
their literacy skills, and is ideal for young readers, reluctant readers and especially
children with dyslexia.

Picture acknowledgements
All reasonable efforts have been made to ensure the reproduction of content
has been done with the consent of copyright owner. If you are aware of
any unintentional omissions please contact the publishers directly so that
any necessary corrections may be made for future editions.
Getty Images: Markus Essler 19.